READ THE TAROT
IN 7 DAYS

A complete course for learning to use the Tarot for divination in just 7 days

Keith Morgan

FIRST EDITION   Eostre (March) 1991ev
Second Edition Lughnasadh (August) 1992ev

Read the Tarot in 7 days
ISBN NUMBER : 1 872189 90 3

PUBLISHED BY PENTACLE ENTERPRISES

PENTACLE ENTERPRISES
BM PENTACLE
LONDON WC1N 3XX

CONTENTS

INTRODUCTION   1

WHAT IS A TAROT   2

THE HISTORY OF THE TAROT   4

CHOOSING YOUR TAROT   6

THE MEANINGS OF THE TAROT   10

THE MAJOR ARCANA   11

THE MINOR ARCANA   15

HOW TO SHUFFLE TAROT   21

PREPARING TO READ TAROT   22

READING THE TAROT WITHIN 7 DAYS   25

READING THE CARDS
& DISPLAYING LAYOUTS   28

DIFFERENT LAYOUTS   30

FINAL WORDS   33

ABOUT THE AUTHOR

Keith Morgan was born in Cheshire in 1961. He studied various Occult teachings from the age of 11 & was initiated into the craft of the wise in 1977.

He continues to work as a practising High priest of Wicca, & as a publisher & author in many esoteric fields. He writes in a simple & concise style which is easily understood by both the initiate & the student of the occult arts.

Keith is proud & outspoken about his beliefs, he has given interviews on local & national TV & radio & continues to be in the forefront of developing new ideas about all Occult teachings & paths.

Keith is also the editor of The Deosil Dance, the most radical of all Pagan & occult magazines around today

Anna Greenwood

INTRODUCTION

The Tarot is a Mirror. A Mirror that can reflect inner feelings & emotions, it can project future thoughts & ambitions, & place them in a situation in the present where they can easily be understood.

This use of a set of ancient symbology, has lended the tarot to be much maligned through out its history, often because of bigotry, Intolerance & fear, instilled by an established religion, who see the free thinking tolerance of Metaphysical (Occult) practises, as some threat to their own existence.

The tarot is a set of ancient & magickal symbols, it is not a 'Devils Picturebook'; It does not release demons into a persons life, It helps a person to analyse their own situation & its relation to their own life, & even more importantly, how can they reflect this guidance into their future lives & act upon it to a greater effect.

Rather than as a fortune telling aid, look upon the Tarot as being a 'dumb counsellor', someone that you can turn to for guidance & assistance, someone that will listen, & will give aid, freely & without prejudice, & what's more - will be confidential!

The study of the tarot can be a lifetimes work, & there are many very intellectual discourses on this great work, some which have taken a lifetimes study, but that is not the purpose of this book.

The sole purpose of this book, is to give a hands on approach to the absolute beginner, in bringing the art of Tarot reading into accessibility for the beginner.

Tarot reading is not difficult. What is difficult is trying to relate an ancient symbolism to a modern situation, again in this book I hope to put forward a thesis, in which I can show the beginner how, within a period of just 7 days, they too can start to read the tarot for themselves & their families, with confidence & with skill.

WHAT IS A TAROT

The modern concept of what is commonly known as a tarot deck, is a set of cards that is divided into two sections, THE MAJOR ARCANA & THE MINOR ARCANA.

The Major Arcana is a set of 22 cards, the minor Arcana 4 suits of 14 cards, both with the titles given below.

The Major Arcana are often associated as being 'The' definitive Tarot, in that they are often associated as being the original cards, however, as the earliest tarot decks, depict a minor Arcana as well, it should be recognised that the tarot is a complete set of cards as being a major & minor Arcana & should be used as such.

The card description below are faithful to the Rider Waite & associate packs, which are recommended with this book, in other specialised packs, the titles of individual cards may change to suit the intention of the tarot, but most remain faithful to what may be recognised below as the tarot

THE MAJOR ARCANA

0 THE FOOL
1 THE MAGICIAN
2 THE HIGH PRIESTESS
3 THE EMPRESS
4 THE EMPEROR
5 THE HIEROPHANT
6 THE LOVERS
7 THE CHARIOT
8 STRENGTH
9 THE HERMIT
10 THE WHEEL OF FORTUNE
11 JUSTICE
12 THE HANGED MAN
13 DEATH
14 TEMPERANCE
15 THE DEVIL
16 THE TOWER
17 THE STAR
18 THE MOON
19 THE SUN
20 JUDGEMENT
21 THE WORLD

THE MINOR ARCANA

The Minor Arcana is like a set of playing cards in that it is a set of cards numbered 1 -10, plus a royal family of Page, Knight, Queen & King.

The cards numbered 1 -10, are indicative of a situation, or a lesson or parable to be observed, whereas the family cards are definitely cards of recognition. This means that the Royal family in a minor Arcana suit indicate a particular type of person, recognised by their age, & skin & hair colouring.

The Minor Arcana cards are described thus, indicating for example the suit of wands

ACE OF WANDS
TWO OF WANDS
THREE OF WANDS
FOUR OF WANDS
FIVE OF WANDS
SIX OF WANDS
SEVEN OF WANDS
EIGHT OF WANDS
NINE OF WANDS
TEN OF WANDS
PAGE OF WANDS
KNIGHT OF WANDS
QUEEN OF WANDS
KING OF WANDS

THE HISTORY OF THE TAROT

The history of the tarot is set in two sections, the historical basis of which the tarot has been born, & the history of the symbolism contained within the tarot. That historical context of the origin of the tarot has its roots in Medieval Europe, the history of the symbolism contained within it, goes back to the magick of the very dawn of time.

In a genealogical sense, mythology has it that 'Gipsies' brought the tarot, from India, via Egypt & into Europe, & it is interesting to note that the appearance of the early forerunners, of what we know as the Tarot, were emerging in areas of Gypsy encampment, such as Romania, Hungary & France.

The earliest examples of Tarot appeared in Europe in the Twelfth century, & quickly became a game for courtiers, though not in all countries, what may have been seen as harmless fun in France, was strictly forbad by King Edward IV in England, not because they were seen as evil in any way, but because they were seen as inherently French!

The Tarot of the Courtesans of the Middle ages, was not used in a divinatory method, as we know it today.

The court tarot's of the Middle ages, were nothing more than an extension of what we know as a conventional pack of cards, with four suits, 10 pip cards etc, but with the addition of a 'Page card' to the royal suites, & a varied set of 'Trump cards'.

This may be seen as being traditionally known as the tarot, with the very important difference, that the trump cards of the middle ages, were used in card games of chance, as trump cards for advantage over an opponent (as in whist today).

Their association with divination & what is loosely termed the 'Occult' occurred at the end of the Fifteenth century, when an occult philosopher Jacques Gringonneur, Court Astrologer to Charles VIth of France, devised a set of Tarot, based upon the courtiers cards, but with astrological & cabbalistic associations, & its is reputed that courtiers started a form of divination with these cards.

The history of the Tarot becomes somewhat blurred at this point, but their interest re-emerges in the 18th century, when Count De Gbelin, rediscovered the more antiquated forms of the tarot, & gave an association with the Pagan Mystery religions of the Egyptians, thus reinforcing the ancient legends of the Gypsies (the word Gypsy, coming from E-GYP-Tians), & its association with the mystery religions of Isis & Osiris.

The theories of de Gbelin, were well accepted in an atmosphere of the renaissance, where studies into occultism, based upon Rosicrucian, Cabbalistic Classical & Occult inspired legends were at their height, in fact it was De Gbelin's illustrations in his book Le Monde Primitif (The ancient world) that inspired Le tarot Marseille.

The Marseille tarot is the most ancient of what we may consider as to be authentic tarot, in that it has in its composition what we could consider as being a Tarot in which we recognise, in that it has the full set of 22 'Trump' cards

Other occult scientists converted a lot of De Gbelin's work, in particular a French fortune teller Ettelia, who altered De Gbelins original ideas, & gave a closer association with Cabbalistic correspondences

It was in the 19th century, that many occultists gave their own interpretations of Tarot symbology, creating their own symbolic designs, including Eliaphas Levi, Papus, & Oswald Wirth, the latter two creating & devising their own tarot decks

The most modern version of the tarot, & what has without doubt been the easiest form of tarot to use, was created in 1910, By artist Pamela Coleman Smith, under the direction of Arthur Edward Waite, a member of the Occult group, The Hermetic order of the Golden Dawn.

This tarot has the authentic 22 trumps, & 4 suits of 14 cards based upon occult inspired symbology, it is more commonly known as the Rider Waite tarot.

There are now well over 300 different interpretations of the Tarot to choose from, some Esoteric, some very simplistic, when learning to read the Tarot, it is important to choose the correct deck for you, so in the next chapter, we will discuss, choosing your Tarot.

CHOOSING YOUR TAROT

Since the publication on a wide scale of the Rider Waite Tarot, many occultists have created their own Tarot Decks, including Occultist & misunderstood genius Aleister Crowley, who directed Lady Frieda Harris into creating a very psychedelic work based upon his own philosophies, which was in vast contrast to the simplistic designs of The Rider Waite pack.

The Crowley tarot is a work of genius on many levels, but is not one that is recommended to a beginner (& definitely not one for reading within 7 days!), it is a very specialised work, & one that could be encountered, once a familiarity has been obtained with an easier tarot to understand

There are many, many, different Tarot's, as diverse, as the philosophical thinking behind each interpretation, & this is a welcome for the person choosing a particular type of tarot - It is also a problem for the beginner, who can be extremely confused by this array.

Many new interpretations, have their base of originality in The Rider Waite tarot, which has been reinterpreted over many years, & has many derivations, some more stylised, some more simplified, all are excellent for use with is book.

The different Tarot's can be divided into two sections.

PICTORIAL TAROT
A pictorial tarot is defined by the minor Arcana cards, being portrayed as a series of montages, or pictures, giving an immediate description of the meaning of the card.

PIP TAROT
A 'Pip' Tarot, shows the Minor Arcana as being a series of symbols, not too dissimilar to a standard playing card set, with say, The Four of hearts being shown as 4 hearts, so it is with Pip tarot, a card portraying the 3 of swords is shown as being 3 swords, Illustrations of both pictorial & pip tarot are shown overleaf

 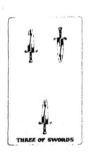

Pictorial tarot   Pip Tarot

Pictorial tarot are very much more recommended for a beginner rather than a Pip tarot, as, the Pictures within a pictorial tarot, are less confusing for the beginner, & the meanings of each individual card can lodge within the subconscious far easier than a Pip card would ever do.

PICTORIAL TAROT'S INCLUDE
THE RIDER WAITE TAROT
THE MORGAN GREER TAROT
THE HANSON ROBERTS TAROT
THE NORSE TAROT
THE CONNOLLY TAROT

PIP TAROT INCLUDE
THE PREDICTION TAROT
THE IJJ SWISS TAROT
THE WITCHES TAROT
THE SIMPLIFIED TAROT
THE CELTIC TAROT
THE PRAGER TAROT

As you can see, the use of a title to describe a tarot really does not bear comparison to their suitability for a beginner to get familiarised with the tarot, & tarot described as Witches, Simplified, or prediction, which you would assume would be suitable for a beginner, in reality are not really that suitable, due to them having a Pip system of minor Arcana.

These cards can be used at a later date, but when one has more familiarity with the individual meanings of each of the Cards.

Whilst the Rider Waite pack is used for illustrations within this book, many of the later derivations can also be quite happily used compatibly with this book, these include;

THE MORGAN GREER TAROT
THE HANSON ROBERTS TAROT
THE NORSE TAROT
THE CONNOLLY TAROT
     It is any of these four tarot packs that I would strongly recommend for using with this book.

These Tarot are available from many occult/New Age bookshops, mail order companies, or from where you purchased this book, see the rear of this book for further details.

There are many many more specialised tarot available today, all of which are extremely valid in their own particular ways, many having a sound base in Occult Theology & psychology, but not of great use to the absolute beginner, again, these tarot are well worth experimenting with at a later date, when a greater familiarity has been achieved with the chosen beginners tarot.

SPECIALISED TAROT INCLUDE;
THE CROWLEY TAROT
THE MYTHIC TAROT
THE MERLIN TAROT
THE GOLDEN DAWN TAROT
THE GARETH KNIGHT TAROT
THE KARMA TAROT
THE CAT PEOPLE TAROT
THE HAINDL TAROT
THE SACRED ROSE TAROT

THE SOLLEONE TAROT
THE NATIVE AMERICAN TAROT
THE XULTAN MAYA TAROT
THE EGYPTIAN TAROT
THE MOTHERPEACE TAROT
THE BARBRA WALKER TAROT
THE VOYAGER TAROT
THE TREE OF LIFE TAROT
THE MAGICKAL TAROT
THE MANDALA ASTROLOGICAL TAROT
THE HERMETIC TAROT
THE MASONIC TAROT

A lot of specialised tarot, differ greatly from what the beginner may recognise as being a Tarot, in the meanings of the Minor & Major Arcana's, in that the title of some of the cards may differ from the titles known to be of that particular card, & as such create confusion.

Once again, I must stress these cards are valid, for someone having a working |& confident knowledge of the basics of tarot & are best left alone until a confidence is obtained through a beginners pack.

When you have decided which tarot is the best suited for your purposes, & you have them, it cannot be stressed to much that a need to get to know your cards is an essential requirement for confidence with reading the cards.

Treat the cards with respect, keep them separate from mundane objects, & if possible, keep them wrapped in a natural cloth such as Cotton, Wool or Silk, & keep them in a pouch or box specifically obtained for the purpose.

This is standard procedure with magickal equipment (& Tarot are very much magickal equipment), to show that a respect is give for something out the norm of reality.

This is not an eccentricity for respect over 78 pieces of cards, but more of a respect for the arcane symbology that is upon the cards.

THE MEANINGS OF THE TAROT

The individual interpretative meanings of each of the cards differ from one persons opinion of such to another, what I am giving below is my interpretation of each of the cards, & how I personally can relate to them.

I am not saying they are the definitive interpretation of each of the cards, what I am saying is that they are a set of interpretations which have worked for me over the last 17 years (to date!), & have been used both in a personal & professional capacity for reading the tarot.

The meanings below are given from a psychological analysis of my own, based upon my own Mythological, legendary, Occult & Psychological orientated interpretations of each card & their relation to myself, & the magick that I weave.

The tarot as a whole shows the composite & complex nature that make up the human psyche, & your analysis of it, & remember, that is what using the tarot is about, not for fortune telling, but for the analysis of the individual, & the clear sight (Clairvoyant) analysis of anticipation of future events.

If you disagree with any of my interpretations, then this is fine & I accept this as your own individual progression through the tarot & the relating to each of the cards & their symbolic meanings.

I would always recommend that you keep notes on your studying of the individual cards, & write up any observations that you make of your own.

A NOTE ON REVERSE MEANINGS;

Many authorities regard Tarot Cards as having just one meaning, or which can be even more complicated, of having a reverse meaning that is totally contradictory to the main symbolic meaning of each of the cards.

I have always viewed reverse meanings to be the opposite to the main meaning of the card, therefore, it negates the positive, or replaces a negative meaning with a positive meaning.

This makes more sense when learning to read tarot, than having to learn another 78 different meanings for the meanings of the tarot.

THE MAJOR ARCANA

The major Arcana indicates individuals, situations, or occasions, it is a transition through the personal self development of the tarot, & lessons, or teachings that can be obtained via using the Tarot.

0 THE FOOL
The fool represents the seeker, the lone individual that is starting his journey in search of knowledge or the obtaining of answers. It represents either the reader or the subject of the reading.

1 THE MAGICIAN
A person in control of the 5 elements of nature, Earth, Water, Fire, Air & Spirit, which make up the composite magickal force. It represents a person who is in control & in command of a situation. As they are part of the situation & not divorced from it, they are central in importance to the reading.

2 THE HIGH PRIESTESS
The serene & sincere knowledge of the High Priestess is in contrast to the active magickal attitude of the Magician & is seen to represent that which is already known, that which is in the heart, a feeling of surety in ones actions or beliefs.

3 THE EMPRESS
The Empress is a personification of Mother Nature, a warm & homely loving aura, that surrounds one, It represents a stability & surety within a situation. It is seen as being a Mother Figure, & could represent ones mother, or wife (depending on how one views ones spouse)

4 THE EMPEROR
Stern father figure is prominent within the Emperor card. The sternness is tempered by responsibility & the responsibility instilled within a person. This card could represent a Father figure or husband, (see above),

5 THE HIEROPHANT

A force of spirit, but one that is dogmatic. This card is a representation of establishment, either on a governmental basis, or of an established order, in that it indicates the way in which things should be seen ass being , rather than that which they actually are.

6 THE LOVERS

Very self explanatory in that it indicates a love, or a situation of affection, but if one considers the role of the Angelic force coming between them, it also shows, that a third party could well be central to the disruption of that affection. The third party could well be another person, a situation, or a problem.

7 THE CHARIOT

A natural progression of a situation, a moving forward of events. Could also indicate travel or the opportunity for discovery or adventure.

8 STRENGTH

This is the inner strength that comes from within, not a strength born of force, but rather an inner courage, the courage of ones convictions etc. It can also indicate a determination that transcends the norm.

9 THE HERMIT

An indication of inner knowledge, & the light of such within (the lantern the Hermit carries).

The hermit indicates a situation that is of a personal nature, in that it directly relates to a situation that concerns the person directly, rather than as a generalised situation.

10 THE WHEEL OF FORTUNE

Destiny, or karma is often indicated as a wheel that cannot be stopped, this is this card, it indicates the destiny (or fortune) of an individual or of a situation.

It cannot be overrided, in that this is the way that it was meant to be, therefore, this is the way it is - It is a card of acceptance of a situation, rather than as a lesson to be learned.

11 JUSTICE

Balance, in all matters has to be maintained in a natural & harmonious world, so is it with Justice, it is an indication of natural balance, & is a lesson that balance should be retained.

The balance of the just is not a balance of morality but a balance of opinion, & balance is a lesson to be indicated in all matters.

12 THE HANGED MAN

The hanged man is one of those curious cards within the tarot, that many people indicate as being of a negative nature, & this is not normally so.

The hanged Man is an indication of self sacrifice, in that what is happening is that the reader (or subject of the reading), is showing an element of sacrifice for the good of a situation, they may well be forgoing that which they know is right to maintain a balance, or to restore balance to a situation.

13 DEATH

Like the Hanged Man, very misunderstood, not so much a Death Card, but a card of transition, a card of change in all things & all circumstances. This card should not be feared or ignored, for it is a very important card in that it shows a very great change is about to occur, that will affect the situation very much of the subject of the reader.

14 TEMPERANCE

The Temperance card, again is very much misnamed, for it indicates a renaissance in a situation, a renewal of old ways, once old lessons have been learned. The picture on the temperance card is the symbol of Aquarius, & this card shows, the herald of the New Age, & the new era that is being entered into through the transitory period.

15 THE DEVIL

There is a dualistic approach to the card often known as the devil, as the term devil is one of invention of an unknown term in Christian mythology, so is the card. It shows that which does not really exist, but which one may think does. It indicates, Paranoia, negative imagination, leading towards suspicion, & imagined bondage & struggle.

In fact it could be typified at Kicking out at that which is not really there.

16 THE TOWER
The shedding of materialistic burden in favour of a more spiritualistic outlook. Any disruption to a situation is bound to bring a cleansing to it, & create a harmonious afterlife.

It is the calm after the storm, & an indication of the calm atmosphere that will ensue after a chaotic chain of events.

17 THE STAR
As the New Age brings about a new insight into old situations, so is this, the card of the New Age, the bringing of peace, tranquillity, Good health, & spiritual awareness to a person or situation.

Its appearance within a reading is an excellent indication that new beginnings are starting to manifest themselves for the good of a situation.

18 THE MOON
feminine wisdom, Imagination & intuition are all encapsulated in this card. It is also an indication of the potential, & recognition of psychic abilities, & should be seen as a sign that it is precipitous that these powers should be concentrated upon.

19 THE SUN
Masculine wisdom, Materialistic happiness & wealth, contentment & a good stable family relationship, all that one could ask for! An indication of perfection & the achievement of such

20 JUDGEMENT
The end of a situation, a fulfilment or climax, in that personal energies dispensed upon a project now pay dividends. This could also be an indication of favourable results in legal disputes.

21 THE WORLD
A full completion of a situation or circumstance, it could also indicate a total change of circumstance or situation. It is often taken in a reading as being a signal of liberation, of release of burdens & the fruitful completion to a situation.

THE MINOR ARCANA
The Minor Arcana is divided into 4 suits, & within these suits into 10 pip cards, plus a royal family. The pip cards are indicative of a situation, & the suit cards are indicative of a person, or personality.

SUIT OF WANDS
The suit of wands represent outside influences of all natures that affect the subject of the reader, they also represent lessons to be learned in relation to the other cards falling in relation to cards of the wands suit.

ACE OF WANDS
The indication that outside influences are at work within a situation

TWO OF WANDS
Looking to the future for guidance upon a situation. Regret of things that have gone, but a confidence in future events.

THREE OF WANDS
Creating plans for future events, making plans now that will take effect at a later date, Planning for the future.

FOUR OF WANDS
The hope for a beautiful environment, a happy family homelife & peaceful domestic situation

FIVE OF WANDS
The acknowledgement that future plans could encounter some problems, & a warning of strife that may hinder future plans

SIX OF WANDS
Triumph, success & achievement, the overcoming of adversity for the common good.

SEVEN OF WANDS
Challenging an adversary head on, making a stand for ones own ground, & making sure that ones family & other domestic arrangements are protected. making plans of protection for the future.

EIGHT OF WANDS
News coming from afar, messages or information coming from outside the family situation. It is also indicative of news of a birth or other good or positive news

NINE OF WANDS
Personal Strength in the projection of that which one considers to be valuable. Ensuring that no one takes advantages upon a personal situation

TEN OF WANDS
Moving forward, the carrying forward of ideas or plans for the future. Can also describe a moving of house or home situation, especially if in a position between pentacle cards & cups cards.

PAGE OF WANDS
Indicates a Small Auburn Child

KNIGHT OF WANDS
Indicates an Auburn Youth

QUEEN OF WANDS
Indicates an Auburn Woman

KING OF WANDS
Indicates an Auburn man

SUIT OF SWORDS
The Suit of Swords represents problems or encounters that face the subject of the reading

ACE OF SWORDS
The indication of problems feature strongly within a situation & remedies towards the solving of these problems.

TWO OF SWORDS
A choice, a separating of the ways, if in a question of personal relationships, could indicate a separation, divorce etc.

THREE OF SWORDS
A situation of personal hurt, or emotional stress or strain

FOUR OF SWORDS
The shelving of all plans due to lack of energies, the stagnation of an idea. Lesson to be learnt with this card, is rest & rejuvenation.

FIVE OF SWORDS
The winning of a Battle, a success overcoming a problem, but one which has created hurt within another

SIX OF SWORDS
The moving forward of an idea, travel overseas may feature. In a negative sense it could indicate that a person is moving away to avoid hurt or being hurt.

SEVEN OF SWORDS
Theft & stealth, a mistrust which could create personal problems, because the theft is of something of an important or vital nature

EIGHT OF SWORDS
Bondage or restriction, being in a situation, where someone does not wish to be in. Doing things which is against a persons will.

NINE OF SWORDS
Grief over a loss of a loved one, or loved item. A time of self sympathy, & a time of feeling hollow, because there is something that is felt to be missing within ones life.

TEN OF SWORDS
A violent attitude, leading to danger or despair someone who is in danger. Castigation or excommunication of an individual, the shunning of a person through their hurt to you.

In some extremely rare circumstances, could indicate the death of a person, & this can be noted when all the cards around this are of a very negative nature.

IT MUST BE STRESSED THAT THIS IS RARE, 7 NO ONE WHO TAKES TAROT READING SERIOUSLY WOULD EVER CAUSE GRIEF WITHIN A THIRD PARTY BY TELLING THEM OF SUCH STUPIDITY AS AN IMPENDING DEATH,
there is far too many circumstances to be taken into consideration to regard this meaning as valid.

PAGE OF SWORDS
Indicates a Brown Haired, Swarthy Child

KNIGHT OF SWORDS
Indicates a Brown Haired, Swarthy Youth

QUEEN OF SWORDS
Indicates a Brown Haired, Swarthy Woman

KING OF SWORDS
Indicates a Brown Haired, Swarthy Man

SUIT OF CUPS
The suit of Cups represents concerns of the heart, Love, relationships & emotions

ACE OF CUPS
The indication of matters concerning love & affections, matters of the heart etc, feature strongly within a situation, & observations towards the analysis of these problems.

TWO OF CUPS
Pure & True love between two individuals.

THREE OF CUPS
The three graces, bestowing Love, Wealth & happiness upon a situation.

FOUR OF CUPS
A dilemma, a choice which has to be made to affect a persons love for another. the answer to the problem lies within that persons own love or emotions, in other words, that which they feel within their heart is correct.

FIVE OF CUPS
A lost love & regret for that which is lost, but this is a selfish emotion, for what is being forgotten is that there is still some of that love retained, in memories & past emotions, something which can never be taken away.

SIX OF CUPS
The fruits of love, children, an indication of childbirth, or, depending upon the situation, of a very special gift, a token of love, that will be very much sought & cherished.

SEVEN OF CUPS
Desires, wants, hopes & needs, in each of the seven cups is something that is being sought; Wealth, Power, Love, Dreams, Hopes, Success, & magickal energies.

EIGHT OF CUPS
A great sadness of a love spurned, a love that is being left behind, though no body wishes it, outside situations affect a relationship, & as such break up a relationship, a card of sadness & of mixed emotions.

NINE OF CUPS
A contented person, knowing they are well fed, well clothed, well at ease & well loved!

TEN OF CUPS
The attainment of perfect bliss, happy family life, happy home situation & much love & happiness.

PAGE OF CUPS
Indicates a Blonde Child.

KNIGHT OF CUPS
Indicates a A Blond youth

QUEEN OF CUPS
Indicates a Blonde Woman

KING OF CUPS
Indicates a Blonde Man

SUIT OF PENTACLES

The Suit of pentacles represents matters of Money, finance & commerce.

ACE OF PENTACLES
The indication that finance features significantly in a reading, or that the main purpose of a reading is for a financial answer.

TWO OF PENTACLES
Very limited finances, & a juggling of accounts to maintain a balance, indicates a frugality with finance, so no great waves are made.

THREE OF PENTACLES
Working hard for payment, a strenuous task, but one that is skilfully executed, so that whatever money raised will be well appreciated.

FOUR OF PENTACLES
Miserly & selfish attitudes, which create a binding to a materialistic bondage. The pressure of materialism, is creating a negativity around this card & the situation it features in.

FIVE OF PENTACLES
Poverty & unhappiness, but also neglect, in that any situation of poverty, has not been a sudden impact, but has been warned about & ignored for a great length of time. The lesson of this card is to sort ones finances out immediately, & work towards remedying the situation.

SIX OF PENTACLES
Wealth & Happiness, created out of balance & harmoniously using finances to their best effect. Frugality leading to generosity, a symbol of a comfortable situation well deserved through hard work.

SEVEN OF PENTACLES
Toil, & hard work, making financial plans for future harvests, in that work done now will not show benefits for several months.

EIGHT OF PENTACLES
Analysis of finances, in that a close watch should be made upon financial situations so that they can be best manipulated for future success.

NINE OF PENTACLES
Gifts freely given with Love. An indication of a generous nature, & one that should be looked upon as being a blessing. Gifts bestowed by Fate, karma or the Gods.

TEN OF PENTACLES
Peace, contentment & financial security created by lessons learned through good management of finances from an early stage.

PAGE OF PENTACLES
Indicates a Dark Child

KNIGHT OF PENTACLES
Indicates a Dark Youth

QUEEN OF PENTACLES
Indicates a Dark Woman

KING OF PENTACLES
Indicates a Dark man

HOW TO SHUFFLE TAROT

To shuffle a pack of tarot you are doing 2 things;

Arranging the cards on a subconscious level so that they will display a personal interpretation that is specific for a particular time & pace within a universal scheme of things (Karma)

It impresses upon the particular selection, a set pattern or definitions of a persons psyche, thus creating a rapport between the cards (or more correctly the symbols on the cards), & the reader.

When you first obtain a pack of tarot, they are usually packed in order, that is Major Arcana in correct numerological number selection, then the same for the Minor Arcana.   Before you can use the cards for divination, you must prepare them in a way that removes any fixed order of numerological value to the cards.

The easiest way to do this, is to unwrap your cards, place a clean cloth on a large surface, & then scatter the cards over the surface, you can then gather the cards up randomly, & pack once again into a pack..   This only needs to be done once, or whenever you have arranged your cards to be in a synchronistic format (as in the chapter, WHAT IS A TAROT!)

When using the cards to perform a reading, you must shuffle the cards very thoroughly whilst focusing your attention upon the intention of the reading. Tarot cards tend to be of a larger size & quantity than ordinary playing cards, so a little experience at becoming familiar at this technique is advised.

A thorough shuffle includes shuffling both ways for at least 3 minutes, & when shuffling do not forget to shuffle in a turning motion, so you impress upon the pack a set of cards that are inverted.

When you have finished your reading, do not forget to shuffle thoroughly again to dispel any influences that may be residual within the cards, before packing away.   This ensures future accuracy as well as removing all influences of past readings from the cards.

PREPARING TO READ TAROT

The Most important thing that a person needs to read the tarot is the correct frame of mind!

An utmost confidence in your ability to be capable of reading the tarot is absolutely essential, & it must be encountered, as a much a magickal act as any other form of magickal spell, ritual or ceremony.

There is a natural magickal current that is evident in all forms of magick, & none more so than in the reading of the tarot, & this should be recognised very early on, this way you have the total courage of your convictions, that what you are doing is correct & as such will work!

It is wise that you consult SIMPLE SPELLS FROM A WITCHES SPELLBOOK, (published by PENTACLE ENTERPRISES & available from where you bought this book!), & read up on the magickal implications of Karma, & what is acceptable, what is unacceptable to do concerning Magick & creating an effect upon other peoples lives.

This is important, as guidelines have to be established by practitioners of Magick, as the cause & effect of a persons actions have to be answerable by that person to a higher force, that of Karma, or the Will of the Gods.

There are 5 basic rules to performing a successful magickal act such as reading the tarot;

1; TOTAL FAITH IN WHAT YOU ARE DOING.

This means that you know that what you are doing is correct, right for you, or whoever you are performing the reading for, & that the results of the reading will be accepted & appreciated. It is this confidence in your own abilities where the root of all successful magick lies, for it is your confidence projected through any magickal act that creates a successful magickal act.

It is pointless performing a reading for someone who thinks that what you are doing is party games, it is not. It is a serious committed act of magick, that is potent & powerful, in that what you are doing has the potential to change lives, for good or bad, however you perceive this moral attitude.

You have to believe within yourself, that you have the ability to pull these forces together & bring about change, this is essential for the courage of your convictions in taking what you are doing seriously.

The ability to read Tarot, transcends all religious beliefs, all it takes is a willingness to accept the arcane symbolism of the Cards & to learn to understand the power of the symbolism.

Many Pagans & Witches read the Tarot, & many combine the reading of tarot, with other magickal acts, such as ritual, casting of circles etc.

If you wish to create a simple ritual around your tarot reading, using candles & incense, & if this gives a greater confidence in your abilities, then do it!

A scrying Incense & Blue candles are excellent to give an aura of divinatory energy when using the tarot, either within a ritual, or, for giving a circumstance energy.

For advice on this please consult my book WICCA AWAKENS, (again available from where you obtained this book)

2; BANISH ANY PERSONAL BIAS
Using the tarot is a pure magickal act, do not sully its power, or your ability with the tarot, by selling out to personal prejudice. It is all too easy to read into a reading a situation in which you wish (or do not wish) to happen. To pre-empt a situation is to negate the power of the situation. Read the meanings of the cards & the way they fall, in an unbiased & unprejudiced way.

If the reading is for yourself, divorce yourself from the situation & perceive yourself as reading the Tarot for a third party, thus avoiding any bias that you wish to see within the reading for yourself.

3; REALISE THAT MAGICK IS A NATURAL FORCE
What you are doing is not wrong, it is not harmful, you are not opening yourself up to harmful influences, or satanic involvement, these are false allegations aimed at Occult Practises by extremists within the Christian Church, who see the power & potency of tarot as a threat to their own fragile & shallow beliefs.

Tarot is magick, & magick is a natural fore (again see SIMPLE SPELLS FROM A WITCHES SPELLBOOK, or THE TRUTH ABOUT WITCHCRAFT, available from where you bought this book)

4; INDICATE THE PURPOSE OF THE MAGICK CLEARLY
When you are preparing to do a reading, clear your mind, & state the purpose of the reading in your subconscious in a simplified form, do not be vague, do not be complicated, if it is for a reading for a specific length of time, then visualise this in your subconscious.

5; BE PURE IN MIND & THOUGHT
If you are thinking of doing a Tarot reading for an underhanded purpose, or for some insight on a person without their permission etc, don't even try to start this type of magick!

The laws of Karma, which affect all forms of magick, also include tarot reading, & the laws of karma state that you reap what you sow, in that if you do good, you get good returned threefold; if you wish to work negative magick, or magick for selfish ends, you get the same energies returned threefold, therefore, by not wishing to pervade a persons privacy, you are not impinging upon their personal lives & as such are maintaining a distance, so therefore divorcing yourself from the situation.

READING THE TAROT WITHIN 7 DAYS

The following is a timetable for reading Tarot efficiently within a seven day period. I am not claiming for one instant that you will be proficient within 7 days, if you take the tarot seriously, you will understand that the study of the tarot is a lifetimes work.

Within this timetable, you are able in this seven day period, to get to grips with the rudiments of tarot & with these rudiments, be able to get up & running of doing tarot readings for yourself within this relatively short period of time.

Each of the lessons for the days given below, should, if done properly take between 1 & 5 hours for each of the lessons.

It takes a certain amount of self discipline to pace oneself with these lessons, & whether one does them all at once or over a period of weeks, is entirely up to the individual, & how you can fit the study of the tarot into your everyday life. It is recommended that for at least the first 2 months, that you should handle the tarot everyday, & to get to know the cards .

There is no point deceiving yourself by thinking you are competent by rushing, for the only person that you will be letting down is yourself. If you pace yourself & work competently through the lessons given below, then you will obtain a hands on working relationship with the tarot & be able, within this time span to be proficient at reading Tarot cards

DAY 1
Read this book thoroughly & analyse your tarot cards, noting the style & design of each one.

Familiarise yourself with each of the Cards

Learn to differentiate between a major Arcana card & a Minor Arcana Card. Learn also of the differences between the suits of the Minor Arcana.

DAY 2

Study the meanings of each of the cards, whilst having the particular card in front of you, analyse for yourself if you agree with the meanings given in this book for each of the cards.

Note each of the cards as a complete picture within itself, & analyse each of the pictures, what do you see in each of the pictures, is there something, small & discreet, but something which you consider to be important.

If you disagree with any of the meanings given, write up in your note book, what each card means to you (& this is the most important part, what they mean to you!)

It is perfectly acceptable to dispute my opinions given as being my interpretations, you must make up your own mind (not immediately, but when you disagree), as to how you relate to each of the cards.

Start to familiarise yourself with the cards, learn how to shuffle the cards, & how to take the top card off & place in a reading format, but do not try to read the cards yet!

Get confidence in handling the cards, feel confident that you are happy with handling the cards.

DAY 3

By now you should have a confidence in handling the cards, know what each of the cards looks like on sight, you should know the difference between a Major & Minor Arcana card, & you should know how to place into a reading layout.

It is far too early to be able to expect to know the individual meanings of each of the cards, this comes with time, but now is the time to re-cap, go over things explained above & repeat anything that you are unsure of.

Get to know the cards on a more familiar basis, this can only be done, by shuffling, laying them out in the simple 9 card serpent spread (see chapter on tarot Spreads) & analysing each card & its relationship to its neighbour, using both this book, & your own notebook, give some meaning to each of the cards - in your own words. Relate each card to itself, its neighbour to the reading as a whole, you will be disjointed at first, & again to make the reading scan takes confidence & skill, all this will come with time, repeat all the above exercises

DAY 4

Again go through some spreads, trying 2 or 3 different ones, relate each card to its neighbour, see how you can explain their meanings in the form of a story, not making up a work of fiction, but relating to each of the cards & the circumstance visualised when you started the reading. Write up the results of your spreads

Recapitulate on the meanings of each of the tarot cards, get to know their meanings very well. Do not try to learn off by heart at this stage, parrot fashion learning is very negative, allow your own expressions to emerge through each of the interpretations of the cards

DAY 5

Read the chapter on preparing for reading the Tarot, understand the reasons behind each of the guidelines & try to relate to each of the reasons for these guidelines, & why they are to be followed for successful tarot readings.

Draw a list up of 5 reasons for using the tarot cards, 5 purposes for using the tarot as a means of divination, do not include the reasons given below, these are for day 6

DAY 6

Recapitulate on all the above, go over the meanings that you have either asserted for yourself, or those given in this book, for the meanings of each of the cards, & do spreads for the following purposes.

To enquire as to personal events for the next 6 months, on a monthly basis. To enquire as to personal events for the next 12 months, on a general basis..

To enquire for World events for the next 6 months, on a monthly basis For answering specific questions (assert for yourself what the questions could be, I am sure by now, you will see the potential that Tarot Divination could be put to.

DAY 7 By now, you should be proficient to start reading Tarot on a serious basis, for both yourself & others who may ask you, but please remember, the study of tarot is a lifelong study, & the more that you use it, & become more familiar with each of the cards, the easier it becomes for you to assess the meanings that you can relate to for each of the cards.

READING THE CARDS
& DISPLAYING LAYOUTS

To read the cards you will need to place them out into a spread, the spread should be upon a flat surface, such as a table etc, that is a comfortable height for you to be able to concentrate upon the cards.

A dinner table or desk is an excellent table to read from, as it is of a correct height to be sat at comfortably, as well as having space on it to lay the cards out.

To protect the cards, it is best to cover the table with a cloth, this keeps the cards clean both physically & psychically.

The cloth that you choose should be of natural fibres such as Cotton, wool etc, & should have a non slip surface, velvet is a nice surface to work with, as it is easy to manoeuvre the cards into positions.

The cloth that you use should be of a single colour, so as to not distract you from the meditational values of reading the tarot.

Right, Now you are going to learn to lay your cards out into a spread. This is done in separate stages. Firstly, the preparation, sit at the table you are about to use, with your tarot in their box in front of you.

CLEARING THE MIND;
Clear your mind of interruptive thoughts, & focus your mind upon the single intention of preparing to read the Tarot.

STILL YOUR MIND & BRING ABOUT A PEACE OF MIND ABOUT YOU, THERE IS LITTLE POINT IN READING TAROT AT THIS STAGE IF YOUR MIND IS WANDERING, A SELF DISCIPLINE IS NEEDED TO CONCENTRATE UPON THE ACT TO BE PERFORMED.

Take your tarot out of their box (protective wrap etc)

CONCENTRATE UPON THE INTENTION OF THE READING;
Taking hold of your Tarot, fix the intention of the reading in your mind, & start to slowly shuffle the cards, intentionally concentrating on the purpose of the reading.

PLACING THE CARDS IN THE SPREAD;

When you are happy with the shuffling, & when you feel ready, take the cards from the top of the pack, & place them face down upon the cloth in the shape of the spread to be used.

Return the remainder of the cards to their box.

READING THE CARDS;

Now, starting at the beginning of the spread, turn the first card over so you are able to see it, concentrate upon this card & give the interpretation of the meaning, continue with the second card.

With the second card, observe its relationship with the first card, & look for links with the first card that you have turned over.

Continue, systematically, turning each card over when you come to it, & relate the meaning of each of the cards, to its neighbour & to the whole reading itself.In this way you will build up a pattern for the purpose of the whole reading.

FINISHING THE READING;

When you have finished, collect all of the cards, & with a cleared mind, shuffle the cards to dispel all the influences. Place with the remainder of the cards, not used, & shuffle again to re-integrate the cards to the rest of the pack.

The following layouts are ones that are perfect for beginners to use simply & efficiently, there are a myriad of spreads available, & different readers have different spreads for different purposes, below are a selection of spreads that I would recommend to start with.

DIFFERENT LAYOUTS

THE CELTIC CROSS
This very simple reading is ideal for obtaining information about future developments of a personal nature, that will affect a person or situation

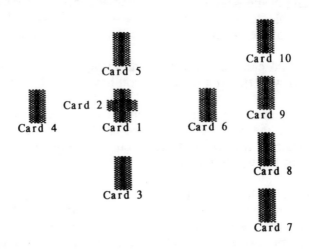

CARD 1; This represents the general atmosphere around the main subject of the reading

CARD 2; This represents the opposing forces, or forces that may bring about a conflict or obstacle to the subject of the reading.

CARD 3; This represents the experience of past influences on the subject of the reading.

CARD 4; This represents the immediate influences that affect the subject

CARD 5; This represents influences for the immediate future

CARD 6; This represents influences for experiences for some time ahead, but ones which will effect the outcome of the reading.

CARD 7; This represents the fears or troubles of the subject of the reading

CARD 8; This represents the immediate environment of the people behind the subject of the reading.

CARD 9; This represents the hopes or wishes or desires of the subject of the reading

CARD 10; This represents the final outcome for the reading

THE TREE OF LIFE SPREAD
This reading is most effective for obtaining information of a personal nature about a subject with their permission), it gives analytical insight into a persons own psyche.

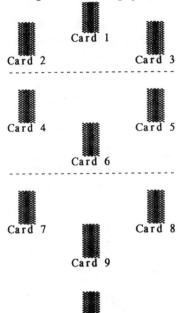

This spread is split into 3 parts each relating to 3 different aspects

TOP THREE CARDS
The spiritual goals of the individual

CENTRAL THREE CARDS
Intellectual & moral indications of the subject of the reading

BOTTOM THREE CARDS
The hopes & anticipations of the subject of the reading

CARD 1; This represents the aims or ideals of the subject of the reading
CARD 2; This represents The creative power of the individual
CARD 3; This represents the wisdom of the subject of the reading
CARD 4; This represents the virtues & qualities of the subject

of the reading

CARD 5; This represents the negative aspects of the subject, ones which could be his downfall

CARD 6; This represents his health, & future prospects for health

CARD 7; This represents the love of things of an esoteric nature, & the abilities to express the emotions of the subject.

CARD 8; This represents outside influences for the subject

CARD 9; This represents the fears of the subject of the reading

CARD 10; This represents the final outcome of the reading

THE SERPENT SPREAD

An ideal spread to start with, & one that gives a person confidence before advancing onto more elaborate readings, it gives a time scale to analyse for a person starting to read the tarot.

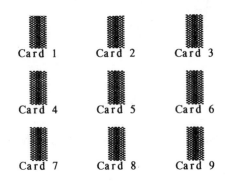

CARD 1; This represents the distant past

CARD 2; This represents the obstacles of the subject of the reading.

CARD 3; This represents the near past

CARD 4; This represents the hopes of the subject of the reading

CARD 5; This represents the Here & Now

CARD 6; This represents the fears of the subject of the reading

CARD 7; This represents the near future

CARD 8; This represents The outcome of the reading

CARD 9; This represents The distant Future

FINAL WORDS

In my work as a professional Metaphysician (you can also use the words, Witch, Shaman, Wise One, Occultist, Magickan, Pagan philosopher etc etc), I am often asked of the validity of Magickal energies, & their validity in a world that is without doubt based upon scientific principles.

How can a set of 78 cards actually foretell what is going to happen to a person? I answer my critics in a way that they understand, in that I too believe in scientific principles, & I am happy to equate magickal technique to scientific principles, I am the biggest sceptic of all, If I cannot see it, feel it touch it, taste it & relate to it, then I will not acknowledge it exists, & this includes magick!

Yet I know that magick as a natural force exists, for I can see it, feel it touch it, taste it & relate to it! Therefore I acknowledge it exists!

Physics tells us life is based upon a series of chance coincidences, & this includes chance selections, this is how the tarot works, in the same way as natural selection, by chance, based upon destiny.

When divining by tarot (Divining meaning being one with the sacred), you are letting your destiny make a chance selection & for this the greater number of cards that one has the more infinite the possibility of eliminating fraud becomes.

To use just the Major Arcana in works of Divination (or more correctly cartomancy), is to use the tarot incorrectly, because you are limiting your options, in a mathematical sense, to use a full set of Tarot, expands your options to the following formula

Using a full 78 card pack;   'Y' x 78()
Using a 22 card Major Arcana 'Y' x 22()
(Y = Amount of Cards in a spread).

The first calculation gives an infinite number of selections, whereas the second calculation gives a selection that is a fraction, one third of one millionth, of a choice.

In other words, the more cards that you use, the greater the passibility of an accurate reading, but also, the less chance there will be of a repetitive interpretation.

Theoretically with a full tarot deck it is possible to perform a reading, every day of ones life & never get a reading the same!

This is even more awesome, when one considers that by using a full set of tarot, you would not get a same reading if you lived to the ripe of age of 400,000 years!

Therefore, the infinite possibilities show that with the accuracy of the Tarot (& believe me, I have experienced the accuracy of the tarot first hand, I have made an extremely successful living out of reading tarot on a professional basis), then the possibilities of eliminating chance guesswork has become replaced by a scientific principle of natural selection based upon natural forces that are guided by Destiny!

1993 MAGICKAL DIARY
£4.95

Due to public pressure I decided to publish a 1993 edition of the Magickal diary, however to ensure that this years diary is the best of all times, it contains a complete Ephemeris for 1993 as well, & at just £4.95, what a Bargain!

It must also be stressed however that I have no intentions of being left with a load of diaries on my hands this year, as happened last year, so there is a limited print run, so if you want one of these diaries, then order it now!

The Magickal diary is a feast of information containing all Pagan festivals from all traditions, Moon phase dates, Zodialogical change-over dates, plus magickal correspondences, magickal hours tables, plus unique to this year, a full & accurate Ephemeris for 1993, for all you astrologers.

Completely updated & added too, this is yet another winner from Pentacle Enterprises, BUT BE ASSURED DEMAND WILL BE HEAVY & NUMBERS ARE LIMITED SO ORDER YOURS NOW!

It's an ideal present for families or friends, so if ordering in bulk please let us know as soon as possible.

DEMAND WILL BE HEAVY SO ORDER YOURS NOW TO AVOID DISAPPOINTMENT - WHEN THEY ARE GONE, THEY ARE GONE!

All prices include Postage & Packing,
please make cheques payable to PENTACLE ENTERPRISES
& send to address below

PENTACLE ENTERPRISES
BM PENTACLE
LONDON WC1N 3XX

INTERESTED IN MAGICK & WITCHCRAFT ?
SUBSCRIBE TO DEOSIL DANCE TODAY!

THE DEOSIL DANCE is a quarterly journal that has been regularly published to promote the old ways in the context of their relevance today. THE DEOSIL DANCE is considered by the Occult community to be thought provoking, revolutionary, controversial, & if this is the case, then it has to be down to the way in which controversial issues are put forward by a myriad of contributors & authors, many of who are famous, & well respected having had their work in print so many times, & are well known within the Pagan/ & Occult Scene . In a well balanced way, there is much for both the beginner, the adept, the curious & the committed, for all points of view are considered from all peoples of all paths.

Published 4 times a year on the Greater Sabbats, it is produced in an extremely high quality glossy hard cover A5 format with a least 40 pages in each issue, which, is amazing value for just £6.00 per year. The advantages for subscribers are immense, not only do you get advance notice of new products etc, but you also get advance notification of unique special offers. As well as a high quality magazine 4 times per year, all subscribers are regularly offered free gifts, special offers, special purchases, plus many other advantages for becoming a subscriber, & supporting us in keeping the Pagan way clear!

PLUS; IN 1993 ALL SUBSCRIBERS ARE GIVEN FREE MEMBERSHIP OF CLAN DEOSIL. Clan Deosil is a magickal order, based upon Pagan ethics & teachings, & subscribers can enrol upon a years course teaching them the basics about Witchcraft & Magick, which has a certificate at the end of it, plus tuition throughout the year.

SUBSCRIBERS ALSO GET A 10% DISCOUNT OFF ALL FUTURE PURCHASES WITH PENTACLE ENTERPRISES.
NOW YOU CAN SEE WHY YOU NEED TO SUBSCRIBE TO THE DEOSIL DANCE, TO KEEP IN TOUCH WITH EVERYTHING THAT IS HAPPENING ON THE OCCULT SCENE!

SUBSCRIPTION APPLICATION

I wish to become a subscriber to THE DEOSIL DANCE Journal, starting from issue number 33 / 34 / 35 / 36 (please indicate which.) I enclose my subscription fee of £6 for 4 issues.

Name...............................

Address............................

....
The latest issue is number 33, with issue 34 published in February 1993.
Please state which issue you would like your subscription to run from,
& send this form along with a cheque or postal order made payable to 'Pentacle Enterprise' to
PENTACLE ENTERPRISES
BM PENTACLE LONDON WC1N 3XX

MAGICKAL BOOKS FOR MAGICKAL PEOPLE FROM PENTACLE ENTERPRISES

Sound Magickal advice at prices everyone can afford, why be taken in by the hype, help is at hand!,All the following books are in stock now!

ARADIA
GOSPEL OF THE WITCHES
C G Leland
Aradia, first published in the late 19th Century, aroused a great deal of interest. It was initially the first source book of the Old Religion The information in the book forms a great deal of ritual material for todays pagans. £5.95

SIMPLE SPELLS FROM A WITCHES SPELLBOOK
This book shows the beginner the easy way how to start to work magick, with Excellent advice for all beginners or those not sure in the practicalities of magick. Plus lots of simple spells to get you started, including how to win the pools! £3.50

THE TRUTH ABOUT WITCH CRAFT
Keith Morgan
This book has been written by a practising witch to allay some of the fears & misconceptions of the general public about Wicca & Paganism. £2.50

WICCA AWAKENS
Keith Morgan
Wicca Awakens is a perfect beginners book, on the practise of witchcraft, that gives all the relevant & vital information that a newcomer to the Old Religion needs. £ 4.95

TRADITIONAL WICCA
Keith Morgan
The complimentary volume to Wicca Awakens; it explores the Wicca raised to greater depths. Going a long way into explaining the true nature & identity of the Old Religions of these lands, through the use of natural magickal technique, ritual & legends. £ 4.95

THE HARMONICS OF WICCA
Keith Morgan
The continuance on from Wicca Awakens & Traditional Wicca, it is, a Balancing process for the Old Religion in the New Age. It is without doubt a coming together of principles that are vital to all Pagan paths. £4.95

RUNE MAGICK
Keith Morgan
RUNE MAGICK has been written for the beginner, or for the person knowing little of the power of the Runes & goes into the history of the runes, the ways of divination as well as the ways of using Rune Magickally £3.50

MAKING MAGICKAL TOOLS & RITUAL EQUIPMENT
Keith Morgan
This book is totally unique & original, It gives the reader all the information that they need for making all of their ritual magickal tools. £3.50

HAVE YOU BEEN CURSED?
Keith Morgan
A serious study into the phenomena of curses & Hexes, to allay peoples fears about these subjects. Contains much vital information for people who think they may be at the receiving end of a curse. £3.50

READ THE TAROT WITIN 7 DAYS
Keith Morgan
This extremely simple book shows how to read the tarot in a very effective & simple manner. Absolutely ideal for anyone having a minimal knowledge of the tarot £3.50

PLANET MAGICK
Keith Morgan
The planets influence our lives in a myriad of ways, our moods, our emotions, our feelings. Learn how to harness this power & channel it to bring about effects on our everyday circumstances. £4.00

ALTERNATIVE WICCA
Keith Morgan
The continuance from HARMONICS OF WICCA & the fourth part in the theology course of Wiccan philosophies & goes into the alternatives that are now open to Wiccans within magickal technique. £4.95

SO YOU WANT TO BE A WITCH
Keith Morgan
This book explains in a simple manner, what it is to be a Witch, whether witches are born or

SO YOU WANT TO BE A WITCH
Keith Morgan
This book explains in a simple manner, what it is to be a Witch, whether witches are born or made, whether the perceptions one holds about witches is correct. £3.50

THE HORNED GOD
Keith Morgan
Maligned, ignored, disrespected, who is the Horned God? How does his presence within our own psyche feature in our everyday lives whether we be male or female? £4.95

SIMPLE CANDLE MAGICK
Keith Morgan
Using candles & Incense to create a Magickal environment in which Magickal energies can be harnessed & utilised for your own personal needs & requests. £3.50

CRYSTAL MAGICK
Keith Morgan
This book covers the Natural magick of Crystals in an easy to understand manner. Vital for understanding the very nature of the Deva's that dwell within all crystals. £3.50

EASY ASTRAL PROJECTION
Keith Morgan
This book gives the facts not the fiction regards this most useful & beneficial of meditational techniques that is available to all. £3.50

A GUIDE TO GETTING YOUR BOOK PUBLISHED
Keith Morgan
This book gives the facts about publishers & their policies, & the way in which you can work around these constraints & get your work into print £2.50

All prices include Postage & Packing, please make cheques payable to PENTACLE ENTERPRISES & send to address below

**PENTACLE ENTERPRISES
BM PENTACLE
LONDON WC1N 3XX**

NEW BOOKS FROM PENTACLE ENTERPRISES

CRYSTAL MAGICK
Keith Morgan £3.50
Well everybody was asking me, when was going to put a book out on the Magick o Crystals, so after much thought decided to pu out my own interpretation of what I considere to be the essential power of Crystals!

Crystals & other semi precious stones exude power of their own, & this power can b harnessed bringing forth the magickal energies This book covers this Natural Magickal forc in an easy to understand & most practical way.

Vital for understanding the Deva's that dwell i the mineral world. Extensively illustrated & containing rituals that you can perform wit your crystals, it is a book that is of immens use to both the practitioner & beginner alike

It may not be to everyone's cup of tea, but it' how I work magick with Crystals & it work for me, so why not for you.

HIGH MAGIC'S AID
Gerald B Gardner £4.95
The reprint of the famous classic work b Gerald B Gardner, which in a fiction forma depicts very imaginatively & vividly the whol aspect of what Wicca is all about.

With this being a total reprint, we also hav reproduced all of the illustrations from th original, including the original illustration of the dust-wrapper.

This edition also includes a new foreword written by Patricia Crowther, which also give an insight into the book & the legend tha Gerald Gardner really was!